EVERYONE HAS SUCH DIFFERENT IDEAS ABOUT PEANUT BUTTER.

IT'S A PRETTY CONTROVERSIAL SUBJECT.

IT'S A PRETTY STICKY SUBJECT.

TRICYCLE PRESS • BERKELEY, CALIFORNIA

Remy Charlip

PEANUT BUTTER PARTY

including **THE HISTORY, USES, AND FUTURE OF PEANUT BUTTER**

THE PAINTINGS AND TITLES
ARE IN WATERCOLOR ON ARCHES PAPER.
TYPE SET IN FRANKLIN GOTHIC BY GARY BERNAL.

LIBRARY OF CONGRESS
CATALOGING-IN-PUBLICATION DATA

CHARLIP, REMY.
PEANUT BUTTER PARTY: INCLUDING THE HISTORY, USES, AND FUTURE
OF PEANUT BUTTER / BY REMY CHARLIP.
P.   CM.
ISBN 1-883672-69-4
1. COOKERY (PEANUT BUTTER) 2. PEANUT BUTTER. I. TITLE.
TX814.5.P38C43 1999
641.6'56596—DC21
98-43378 CIP

TRICYCLE PRESS
P.O. BOX 7123
BERKELEY, CALIFORNIA 94707
WWW.TENSPEED.COM
PRINTED IN SINGAPORE
1 2 3 4 5 6 7 8 9 10
99 00 01 02 03 04 05

I LIKE PEANUT BUTTER ALL DIFFERENT WAYS,
WITH APPLES, ICE CREAM, SPAGHETTI, AND PICKLES.

I PREFER A GLOB OF PEANUT BUTTER IN CHOCOLATE MILK.

TOO MANY OTHER THINGS GET IN THE WAY OF THE TASTE.

I COULD NOT HAVE DONE THIS BOOK
WITHOUT THE IDEAS OF MY FRIENDS
JULES BECKMAN, LISA WEIMER, AND JOHN INGLE,
AND HOURS OF DEVOTED HELP FROM MIKA KIMULA
AND MY ASSISTANT/COLLABORATOR, ERIC DEKKER.

THE TALK BY THE CHILDREN
ON THE LEFT-HAND PAGES COMES FROM ACTUAL RESPONSES
CHILDREN GAVE TO QUESTIONS ABOUT
THE HISTORY, USES, AND FUTURE OF PEANUT BUTTER.

SOME IDEAS SOUND LIKE FUN,
BUT I HOPE I NEVER HAVE TO GIVE MY DOG
A PEANUT BUTTER BATH TO GET RID OF A SKUNK SMELL.
OF COURSE, IT MIGHT BE WORTH A TRY, IF ALL ELSE FAILS.

THE PEANUT BUTTER PLAY DOUGH
AND THE PEANUT BUTTER SMOOTHIE ARE BOTH GOOD.
THEY HAVE BEEN KITCHEN-TESTED.
SOME IDEAS I'M NOT BRAVE ENOUGH TO TRY,
SUCH AS THE PEANUT BUTTER REMEDY FOR BURNT PEAS.
SO, YOU ARE ON YOUR OWN. YOU DECIDE.
READ THIS BOOK WITH A GRAIN OF PEANUT BUTTER.

THIS BOOK IS DEDICATED TO ERIKA BRADFIELD,
WHO BROUGHT ME BACK TO THE CHILDREN'S BOOK WORLD
AFTER AN ABSENCE OF TWELVE YEARS.
ERIKA INTRODUCED ME TO DAVID HINDS,
WHO INTRODUCED ME TO PHIL WOOD
AND NICOLE GEIGER, WHO INTRODUCED ME TO
MARY ANN ANDERSON, JENNIFER RIGGS,
AND ANNA ERICKSON, WHO INTRODUCED ME TO
KIRSTY MELVILLE, JONATHAN CHESTER, AND AMY CLEARY.
WITH THIS, MY FIRST NEW TRICYCLE BOOK,
I FEEL I'M IN A SAFE HARBOR
AND HAPPY WITH MY NEW TRICYCLE FAMILY.

Remy Charlip

I LIKE TO ROLL BREAD AROUND IT.

I LIKE IT ON TOAST. THAT WAY IT DOESN'T RIP HOLES IN YOUR BREAD.

I LIKE TO CRUMBLE BREAD IN A BOWL, MUSH PEANUT BUTTER IN IT, THEN ADD SOME JELLY.

I LIKE TO LICK MY FINGERS.

GHOST TOAST PARTY

PUNCH HOLES OUT OF THE BREAD WITH CAP OR TOP OF A SMALL JAR OR BOTTLE.

YOU CAN BITE
THE HOLES
OUT OF ANY
SLICE THAT
YOU EAT
YOURSELF.

TOAST
THE BREAD.

COVER
WITH
PEANUT
BUTTER.

IF YOU
WANT IT
WHITE,
COVER
WITH
CREAM CHEESE.

KETCHUP
MAKES GOOD BLOOD.

FOR HALLOWEEN
YOU CAN MAKE A SKULL
WITH MINI-MARSHMALLOW TEETH.

HERE IS MY FAVORITE: BANANAS OVER PEANUT BUTTER OVER BREAD.
SMOTHER IT WITH MAYONNAISE, MARSHMALLOW TOPPING, AND CHOCOLATE SPRINKLES.
THEN TOAST IT IN THE OVEN. TRY IT. IT'LL KNOCK YOUR SOCKS OFF.

I LIKE IT SIMPLE, JUST PEANUT BUTTER, BREAD, AND SALAMI.

THE BEST WAY IS TO FIRST SPREAD PLAIN BUTTER ON THE BREAD,
THEN PEANUT BUTTER, THEN TOP IT WITH WHOLE PEANUTS.

THAT'S A PEANUT PEANUT BUTTER BUTTER SANDWICH.

NAME GAME PARTY

CUT THE LETTERS OF YOUR GUESTS' NAMES OUT OF BREAD SLICES,
COVER WITH PEANUT BUTTER, AND DECORATE EACH NAME DIFFERENTLY.

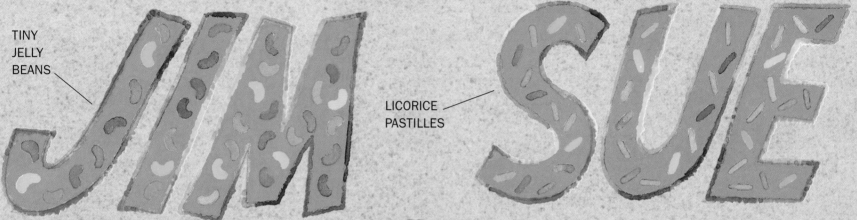

TINY
JELLY
BEANS

LICORICE
PASTILLES

CHOOSE ONE TOPPING
FOR EACH NAME:
CHOCOLATE OR
RAINBOW SPRINKLES,
CANDY CORN,
CHOCOLATE CHIPS,
NUTS, SESAME SEEDS,
RAISINS, POPCORN.
PUT ALL THE DECORATED
LETTERS ON A BIG TRAY.

AT EATING TIME
GUESTS CAN PICK
THE MATCHING
LETTERS
OF THEIR NAME
AND PUT THEM ON
THEIR OWN DISH.
THEY CAN EAT
THEIR WHOLE NAME
OR TRADE LETTERS WITH OTHER GUESTS.

IF YOU WANT A LOOSE TOOTH OUT, ONE THICKLY SPREAD PEANUT BUTTER SANDWICH WITH LETTUCE WILL GET IT OUT.

THAT'S GROSS!

I'VE JUST HEARD IT'S A SURE CURE FOR HICCUPS. IT CLOGS UP YOUR THROAT SO THE HICS WON'T COME UP. IT WORKS ALMOST ALL THE TIME.

I LIKE WATCHING MY DOG EAT IT. A SPOONFUL TAKES ABOUT HALF AN HOUR.

ART GALLERY PARTY

HAVE BREAD, PEANUT BUTTER, AND OTHER INGREDIENTS READY FOR YOUR GUESTS TO MAKE AN EXHIBITION OF ALL KINDS OF PAINTINGS YOU CAN EAT. MAKE A PORTRAIT (PERSON), A LANDSCAPE (PLACE), OR A STILL LIFE (THING).

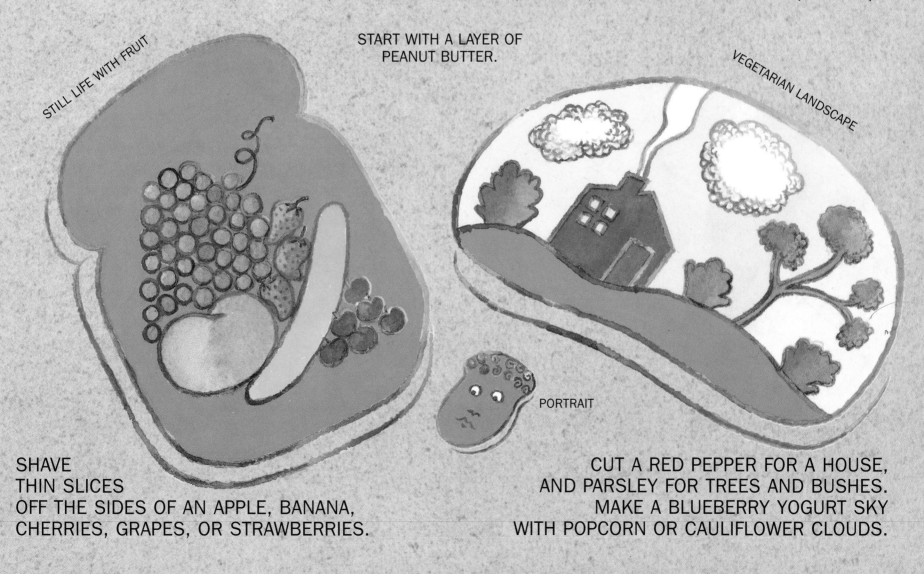

STILL LIFE WITH FRUIT

START WITH A LAYER OF PEANUT BUTTER.

VEGETARIAN LANDSCAPE

PORTRAIT

SHAVE
THIN SLICES
OFF THE SIDES OF AN APPLE, BANANA, CHERRIES, GRAPES, OR STRAWBERRIES.

CUT A RED PEPPER FOR A HOUSE, AND PARSLEY FOR TREES AND BUSHES. MAKE A BLUEBERRY YOGURT SKY WITH POPCORN OR CAULIFLOWER CLOUDS.

WHEN YOUR DOG OR CAT GETS MESSED UP WITH A SKUNK, A PEANUT BUTTER BATH WILL GET RID OF THE STINKY SMELL.

REALLY? I HEARD A TOMATO JUICE BATH GETS RID OF THE SKUNKY SMELL.

THE PEANUT BUTTER BATH SOUNDS LIKE MUCH MORE FUN.

MORE ART GALLERY FUN

YOU CAN MAKE A LANDSCAPE, SEASCAPE, SKYSCAPE, DREAMSCAPE.

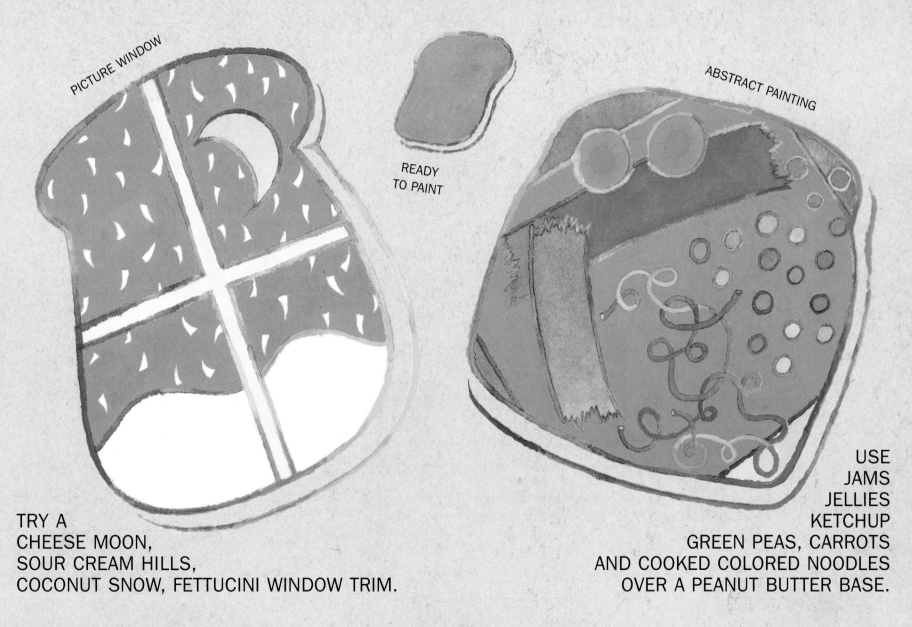

PICTURE WINDOW

READY
TO PAINT

ABSTRACT PAINTING

TRY A
CHEESE MOON,
SOUR CREAM HILLS,
COCONUT SNOW, FETTUCINI WINDOW TRIM.

USE
JAMS
JELLIES
KETCHUP
GREEN PEAS, CARROTS
AND COOKED COLORED NOODLES
OVER A PEANUT BUTTER BASE.

IF YOU'RE OUT OF GLUE, YOU CAN USE PEANUT BUTTER,
BUT DON'T DEPEND ON IT ALL THE TIME.

IT CAN BE USED TO CHANGE THE FLAVOR OF BURNT PEAS.

AND IT DOESN'T SMELL UP THE HOUSE LIKE OTHER FOODS DO.

IT DROWNS OUT ANY BAD TASTE IN YOUR MOUTH.

PEANUT BUTTER UNDER GLASS

YOU CAN HAVE YOUR OWN SCULPTURE SHOW AND EAT IT, TOO.

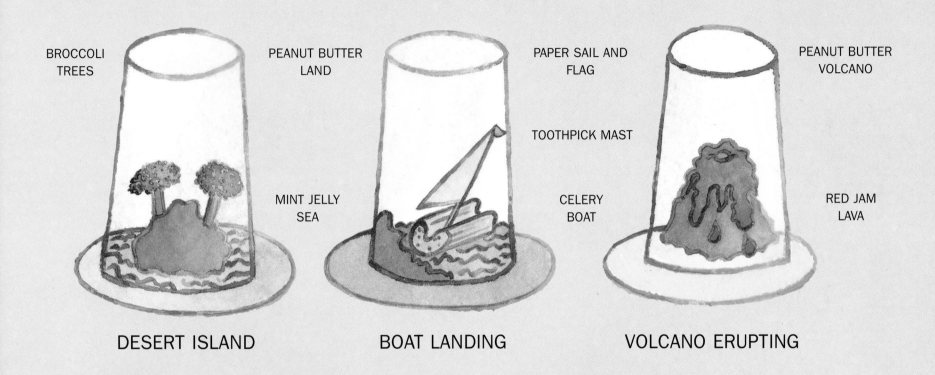

BROCCOLI TREES

PEANUT BUTTER LAND

MINT JELLY SEA

DESERT ISLAND

PAPER SAIL AND FLAG

TOOTHPICK MAST

CELERY BOAT

BOAT LANDING

PEANUT BUTTER VOLCANO

RED JAM LAVA

VOLCANO ERUPTING

PUT A LITTLE LUMP OF STIFF PEANUT BUTTER ON A DISH AND STICK BROCCOLI
IN IT FOR TREES, OR DO A BOAT SCENE WITH CELERY, OR A VOLCANO
WITH RED JAM AS LAVA. YOU CAN MAKE ANY KIND OF SCULPTURE.
THEN TURN A CLEAR GLASS UPSIDE DOWN OVER YOUR WORK OF ART,
JUST LIKE THEY DO WITH SCULPTURE IN AN EXHIBIT CASE IN MUSEUMS.

DID YOU KNOW THAT PEANUT BUTTER CAN REMOVE STUCK BUBBLE GUM?

NO, BUT I'VE HEARD IT CAN BE USED AS FISH BAIT AND MOUSE BAIT.

WHAT A TRAGIC WAY TO USE PEANUT BUTTER.

MEALS ON WHEELS PARTY

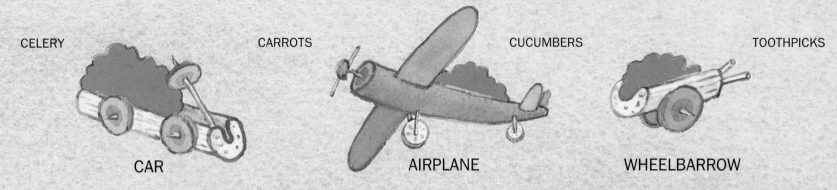

CELERY	CARROTS	CUCUMBERS	TOOTHPICKS
CAR	AIRPLANE	WHEELBARROW	

FINGER FOOD PARTY

PEANUT BUTTER COMBINATIONS

CELERY STICKS • PICKLE SLICES • POTATO CHIPS • TOMATO SLICES • BOLOGNA • BREAD ROLL-UPS • CARROT ROUNDS

CAMOUFLAGE SURPRISE PARTY

WET YOUR HANDS TO MAKE THE BALLS LESS STICKY

COVER POPCORN	A STRAWBERRY	NUTS	CHOCOLATE CHIPS	AN OLIVE

HAVE GUESTS FIRST GUESS, THEN EAT TO FIND A HIDDEN TREASURE IN A GLOB OF PEANUT BUTTER.

I LIKE TO SPREAD THICK PEANUT BUTTER ON BREAD,
THEN CLEAR A HOLE IN THE MIDDLE FOR A LAKE OF HONEY.
IT DOESN'T DRIP OUT THAT WAY.

I HEAR THAT PEANUT BUTTER IS WHAT AMERICANS MISS THE MOST
WHEN THEY ARE IN A FOREIGN COUNTRY.

I FEEL SORRY FOR ANY COUNTRY THAT HAS NO PEANUT BUTTER.

AN INTERNATIONAL PARTY

FOR EACH OF THESE, USE A PEANUT BUTTER SPREAD. THEN ADD OTHER INGREDIENTS.

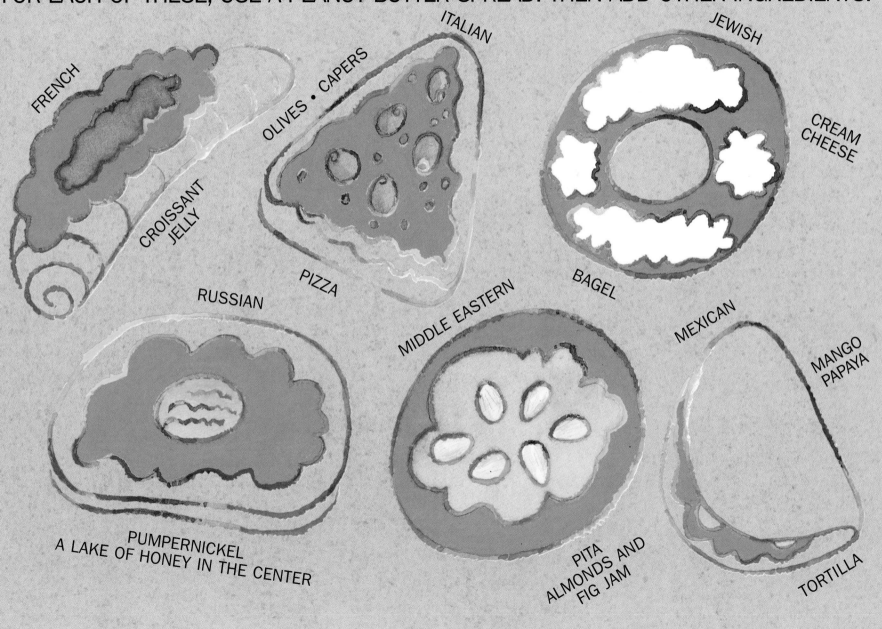

FRENCH

CROISSANT
JELLY

ITALIAN

OLIVES • CAPERS

PIZZA

JEWISH

CREAM
CHEESE

BAGEL

RUSSIAN

PUMPERNICKEL
A LAKE OF HONEY IN THE CENTER

MIDDLE EASTERN

PITA
ALMONDS AND
FIG JAM

MEXICAN

MANGO
PAPAYA

TORTILLA

WHOEVER INVENTED PEANUT BUTTER WAS A GENIUS.

IT WAS MY FRIEND JUNIE MOON. SHE WAS HAVING A PARTY.
HER BEADS BROKE, FELL INTO THE PARTY FOOD, AND RUINED IT ALL.
SO INSTEAD, SHE MASHED UP SOME PEANUTS
AND SPREAD IT ON SOME CRACKERS.

THAT DOESN'T SOUND LIKE A TRUE STORY TO ME.
ANYWAY, I WISH I HAD SOME PEANUT BUTTER RIGHT THIS MINUTE.

PEANUT BUTTER SMOOTHIE IN A ROLL BOWL

DIG A HOLE IN A ROLL UNTIL IT BECOMES A BOWL.

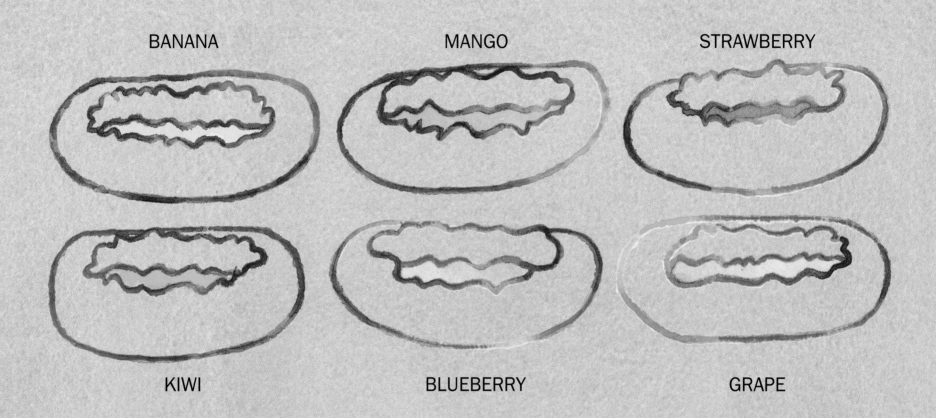

BANANA   MANGO   STRAWBERRY

KIWI   BLUEBERRY   GRAPE

GIVE EACH GUEST A HARD ROLL AND ASK THEM TO DIG A HOLE ON THE TOP.
BE VERY CAREFUL NOT TO DIG INTO THE BOTTOM OR THE SIDES.
ASK EACH GUEST TO CHOOSE THE KIND OF SMOOTHIE THEY LIKE.
ICE CREAM? SHERBET? MILK? RICE DRINK? APPLE? BANANA? STRAWBERRY? GRAPE? PINEAPPLE?
ADD TWO BIG LUMPS OF PEANUT BUTTER INTO THE BLENDER WITH THE SMOOTHIE. BLEND.
POUR INTO THE ROLL BOWLS. SPRINKLE THE TOP WITH CHOCOLATE OR RAINBOW SPRINKLES.

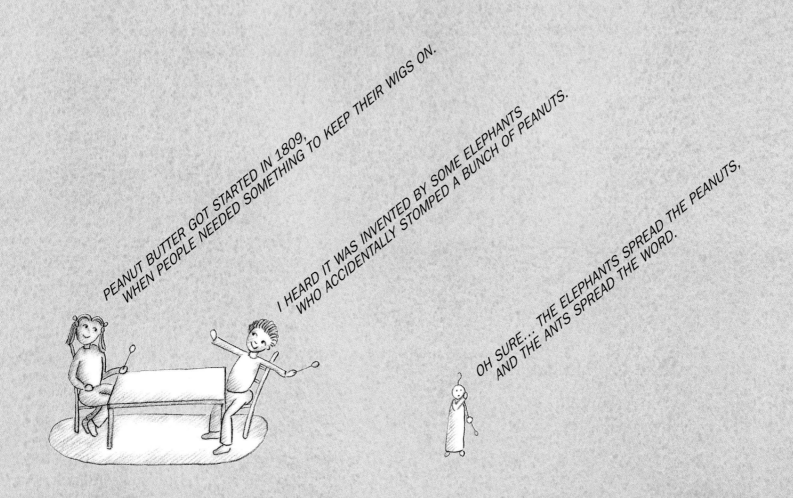

PEANUT BUTTER GOT STARTED IN 1809, WHEN PEOPLE NEEDED SOMETHING TO KEEP THEIR WIGS ON.

I HEARD IT WAS INVENTED BY SOME ELEPHANTS WHO ACCIDENTALLY STOMPED A BUNCH OF PEANUTS.

OH SURE... THE ELEPHANTS SPREAD THE PEANUTS, AND THE ANTS SPREAD THE WORD.

MONSTERS YOU CAN EAT

FIRST MAKE SOME EDIBLE PEANUT BUTTER PLAY DOUGH:
MIX 1 CUP OF CREAMY PEANUT BUTTER WITH 1¼ CUPS
OF INSTANT POWDERED MILK AND 1 TABLESPOON OF HONEY.
THE DOUGH IS EASIER TO WORK WITH AFTER YOU CHILL IT
IN THE FRIDGE FOR AN HOUR OR SO.
MAKE SOME SCARY ANIMALS…
WITH TWO HEADS OR FIVE LEGS OR…

YOU CAN ALSO MAKE OUTER-SPACE CREATURES, BUGS, DINOSAURS, OR ANY IMAGINARY CHARACTERS.
DECORATE THEM WITH RAISINS, NUTS, PUFFED RICE, AND ALL KINDS OF SMALL CANDIES.

ONE OF MY EARLIEST MEMORIES AS A KID WAS GETTING CAUGHT WITH ONE HAND IN A JAR OF PEANUT BUTTER AND ONE HAND IN A JAR OF JELLY.

HOW ROMANTIC!

COSTUMES, SONGS & DECOR

I'M CREAMY.

YOU'RE DREAMY!

MY HEART STARTS TO SPUTTER.

WHEN I'M WITH PEANUT BUTTER.

I'M CHUNKY.

YOU'RE HUNKY!

SMOOTH

NUTTY

IF MY HEADS MIXED UP
OR MY BRAIN'S GONE DEAD
I GET FIXED UP
WHEN MY BELLY'S FED...

(EVERYBODY)
PEANUT BUTTER PEANUT BUTTER
SPREAD ON BREAD

WHENEVER I'M TOLD
"GO STRAIGHT TO BED!"
I'M SURE I'LL SLEEP BETTER
IF MY STOMACH'S FED

(EVERYBODY)
PEANUT BUTTER PEANUT BUTTER
SPREAD ON BREAD

"THANK YOU, THANK YOU,"
MY BELLY SAID
WHEN I SPREAD RED JELLY
ALL OVER MY...

(EVERYBODY)
PEANUT BUTTER PEANUT BUTTER
SPREAD ON BREAD

YOU CAN USE SOME OF THE IDEAS BY THE CHILDREN IN THIS BOOK,
AS WELL AS YOUR OWN IDEAS, TO MAKE UP PLAYS, SONGS, STORIES,
DANCES, AND COSTUMES ABOUT HOW PEANUT BUTTER WAS INVENTED
AND ITS HISTORY, USES, AND FUTURE. THEN, WITH FRIENDS, PUT ON YOUR OWN SHOW.

AFTER 11 YEARS OF PEANUT BUTTER
I THOUGHT I'D LOSE MY TASTE FOR IT,
BUT I'M GLAD IT'S STILL IN MY LIFE.

I'M ALWAYS LOOKING FOR NEW WAYS TO EAT IT.

HAVE YOU EVER TRIED STICKING A PLASTIC STRAW IN A JAR OF PEANUT BUTTER
AND SQUEEZING WIGGLY STRINGS INTO YOUR MOUTH?

I'VE LOVED PEANUT BUTTER EVER SINCE I WAS VERY LITTLE.

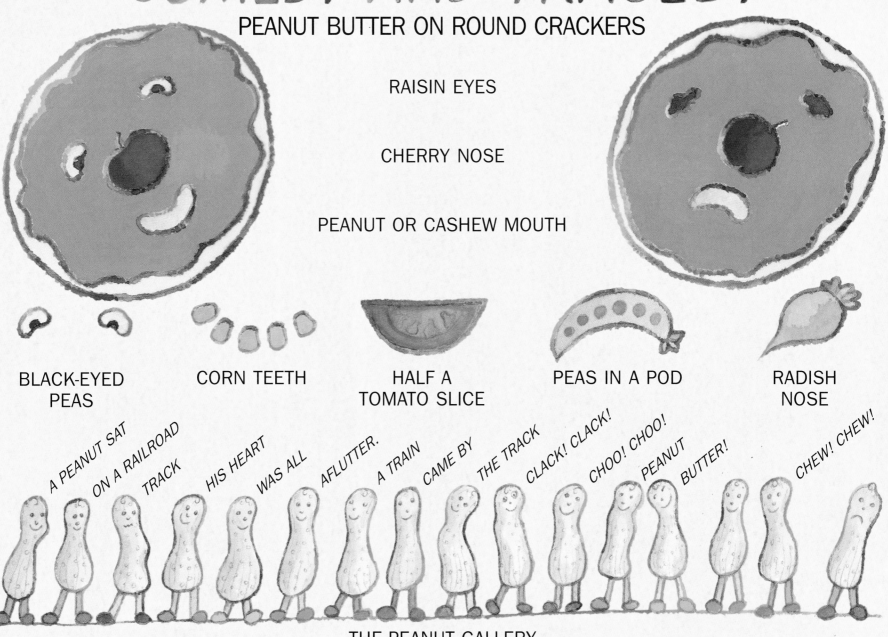

COMEDY AND TRAGEDY

PEANUT BUTTER ON ROUND CRACKERS

RAISIN EYES

CHERRY NOSE

PEANUT OR CASHEW MOUTH

BLACK-EYED PEAS

CORN TEETH

HALF A TOMATO SLICE

PEAS IN A POD

RADISH NOSE

A PEANUT SAT ON A RAILROAD TRACK HIS HEART WAS ALL AFLUTTER. A TRAIN CAME BY THE TRACK CLACK! CLACK! CHOO! CHOO! PEANUT BUTTER! CHEW! CHEW!

THE PEANUT GALLERY

WHEN I WAS LITTLE, ME AND MY SISTER
WERE EACH GIVEN A WHOLE JAR OF PEANUT BUTTER.
I ATE A VERY LITTLE AT A TIME, AND YET,
MY SISTER'S JAR STAYED FULL, AND MINE GOT EMPTIER AND EMPTIER,
UNTIL ONE DAY I CAUGHT MY SISTER WITH _HER_ SPOON IN _MY_ JAR!

I'LL BET YOU WERE MAD.

THAT'S A CLASSIC STORY. I'D BE MAD, TOO!

THE BETTER BUTTER BITTER BATTLE : A PLAY

SMOOTH : I'M THE BETTER BUTTER OF THE TWO.
CHUNKY : THAT'S UNTRUE. YOU TASTE LIKE GLUE.
SMOOTH : I'M REFINED. YOU'RE MUCH TOO NUTTY.
CHUNKY : YOU'RE TOO UNKIND. YOU TASTE
LIKE PUTTY.
SMOOTH : YOU'RE SO GRIMY!
CHUNKY : YOU'RE SO SLIMY!
WHILST I'M A FUNKY, CHUNKY HUNK!
SMOOTH : YOU'RE JUST A PUNKY, CLUNKY LUNK!
IN MY VIEW YOU ARE TOO CHEWY.
CHUNKY : IN MY VIEW YOU TASTE TOO GLUEY.
SMOOTH : YOU'RE TOO ROUGH.
YOU'RE SO UNCOUTH.
TO TELL THE TRUTH,
YOU HURT EACH TOOTH.
CHUNKY : YOU'RE TOO SMOOTH. YOU HAVE
NO CRUNCH. YOU MAKE A BUNCH
OF MUNCHLESS LUNCH.

SMOOTH : YOU'RE A BUMPY, LUMPY CHUMP!
CHUNKY : YOU'RE A SCHLUMPY, GRUMPY CLUMP!
SMOOTH : THIS DUEL IS CRUEL. MUST WE FIGHT?
WHAT IF BOTH OF US ARE RIGHT?
CHUNKY : IT'S SAD BUT TRUE. SOME DO LOVE YOU.
SMOOTH : IT'S TRUE, BOO-HOO.
SOME LOVE YOU TOO.
CHUNKY : SINCE SOME LOVE YOU,
AND SOME LOVE ME,
LET US LET EACH OTHER BE.
SMOOTH : WE POOR JARS
MUST NOW ABIDE
WITH WHAT EACH EATER
DOES DECIDE.
CHUNKY : IN SOOTH
THE EATER NOW MUST CHOOSE,
THE KIND OF GOOEY
CHEWS TO USE.

RIDDLES, GAMES & TRICKS

WHAT DID THE PEANUT GRINDER SAY WHEN QUITTING THE JOB?

"I'M TIRED OF WORKING FOR PEANUTS"

WHAT DOES PEANUT BUTTER SAY WHEN THINGS ARE GOING REALLY WELL?

"I'M ON A ROLL."

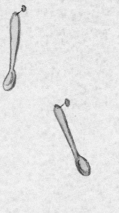

THE PERSON WHO CAN BALANCE A PEANUT ON THEIR NOSE THE LONGEST WINS.

PIN THE SPOON INTO THE JAR

FILL A BIG JAR WITH PEANUTS. THE PERSON WHO GUESSES

HOW MANY PEANUTS ARE IN THE JAR WINS THE JAR.

CUT A PEANUT BUTTER JAR OUT OF PAPER AND PIN IT ON THE WALL.

CUT OUT A PAPER SPOON FOR EACH GUEST. BLIND-FOLDED GUESTS PIN SPOONS ONTO WALL.

THE PERSON WHO PINS THEIR SPOON CLOSEST TO THE JAR WINS.

(A TINY GLOB OF PEANUT BUTTER ON YOUR NOSE HELPS)

I ALWAYS HAVE SOME PEANUT BUTTER AT NIGHT BEFORE I GO TO BED.

I DREAM ABOUT IT AND WAKE UP IN THE MORNING WITH A MAD DESIRE FOR IT.

I WONDER IF JUST THINKING ABOUT PEANUT BUTTER IS WHAT KEEPS ME AWAKE.

BREAKFAST IN BED PARTY

BRING SOME SPECIAL TREATS TO ANY PERSON WHO LIKES TO STAY IN BED.
PUT THE TREATS ON A TRAY AND SAY, "RING-A-LING-A-LING, BREAKFAST-IN-BED PARTY!"

WAFFLES

PANCAKE SANDWICH

FRIENDS TOAST

YOU CAN ALSO ADD FRUIT,
JAM, MAPLE SYRUP, AND HONEY.

I LIKE PEANUT BUTTER WHEN I'VE JUST FINISHED FIGHTING WITH MY BROTHER.
IT CALMS MY NERVES.

EVERY TIME I EAT PEANUT BUTTER
IT STICKS MY TEETH TOGETHER AND I CAN'T OPEN MY MOUTH.
MY SISTER SAYS, "GOOD, STAY THAT WAY."

IT SLOWS ME DOWN AND HELPS CHILL ME OUT
BECAUSE IT TASTES SO THICK.

A QUIET TIME ALL BY YOURSELF PARTY

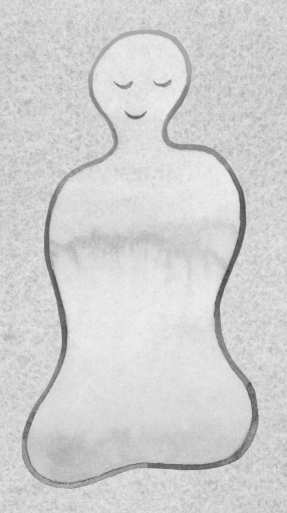

FIND A QUIET PLACE
AND SIT VERY, VERY STILL,
WITH YOUR EYES CLOSED.

WITHOUT MOVING AT ALL,
IMAGINE A JAR
FULL OF PEANUT BUTTER.

NOW, SEE IT SLOWLY,
SLOWLY EMPTYING.

IN YOUR IMAGINATION,
RINSE OUT THE EMPTY JAR
WITH SOAP AND WATER.
THEN DRY IT
WITH A TOWEL.

WITH YOUR EYES STILL
CLOSED,
SEE THE JAR FILL UP AGAIN.

IMAGINE YOU CAN TASTE
A BIT OF IT.

IS IT CHUNKY, OR SMOOTH?

NOW, WITH YOUR EYES
STILL CLOSED
IMAGINE YOUR BODY
SLOWLY EMPTYING.

RINSE IT OUT
WITH WARM SUMMER RAIN.

IMAGINE
A GOLDEN SUN
FILLING YOU UP AGAIN
WITH SPARKLING LIGHT.

SMILE.

YOU CAN ALSO DO THIS WITH A CIRCLE OF FRIENDS.

I DREAM OF A FUTURE WHERE THE WHOLE WORLD WOULD BE MADE OF PEANUT BUTTER.
IT MIGHT BE A LITTLE MESSY, BUT NO ONE WOULD GO HUNGRY.

WITHOUT PEANUT BUTTER, IT WOULD BE A DISASTER.
EVERYONE WOULD HAVE THE TROUBLE
OF THINKING UP OTHER THAN PEANUT BUTTER SANDWICHES FOR LUNCH.

I CAN'T EVEN IMAGINE A WORLD WITHOUT PEANUT BUTTER.